ALL SEGOVIA
AND PROVINCE

7th Edition, January 1988

I.S.B.N.

Spanish	84-378-0002-1
French	84-378-0004-8
English	84-378-0006-4
German	84-378-0008-0

Dep. Legal B. 1376-1988

 **escudo de oro, s.a.** Palaudarias, 26 - 08004 Barcelona - Spain

Impreso en España - Printed in Spain
F.I.S.A. Palaudarias, 26 - 08004 Barcelona

THE ARCHES OF THE AQUEDUCT—WINDOWS ONTO THE HISTORY OF SEGOVIA

This illustrious Castilian city has had a historical identity of its own since very early times. After the Celtic invasion, Segovia became, according to the Marquis of Lozoya, a land "peopled by shepherds and hunters who were good horsemen and bold warriors". It was those same Celts who, modern historical research tells us, were the founders of the city of Segovia around the year 700 B.C. Conquered and destroyed by the Romans about 80 B.C. the city was rebuilt by them and soon became one of the most important imperial Roman cities in the Iberian Peninsula. From its magnificent Roman past Segovia has retained its extraordinary aqueduct; its stone silhouette rises up over the fine land of Castile as an immovable landmark in history.

During the period of domination by the Visigoths, Segovia became the chief town of a bishoprick and then fell into Arab hands; during this time the city lost much of its importance. Later on, however, in the time of Count Raimundo de Borgoña, Segovia recouped much of its lost vitality. During

The stone silhouette of its historic Roman aqueduct is one of the best known and most beautiful views of Segovia.

An aerial view of Segovia with the Roman aqueduct crossing the city.

the reign of Alfonso X the Wise, Segovia acquired the status of a royal court which it kept under some later monarchs.

Between the XII and XIV centuries Segovia became a vigorously active city with notable economic prosperity and a flowering centre of comercial life. Its cattle and wool spinning industry increased considerably and the Council of La Mesta took its wool to Segovia making the city rich and powerful for centuries.

Both John II and Henry IV resided in Segovia for long periods and Isabella the Catholic was proclaimed Queen there in 1474. The city acquired historical importance as it developed and this was specially evident when Segovia became the centre for the "comuneros" who rose against the excessively oppressive royal power in defense of civil liberties and citizens' rights. In spite of the defeat of the "comuneros" Segovia continued to be a vital centre for industry and commerce in Castille at that time. Economic prosperity brought about the building of monasteries and hospitals which helped to further the good works of Saint John of the Cross and Saint Teresa de Jesús.

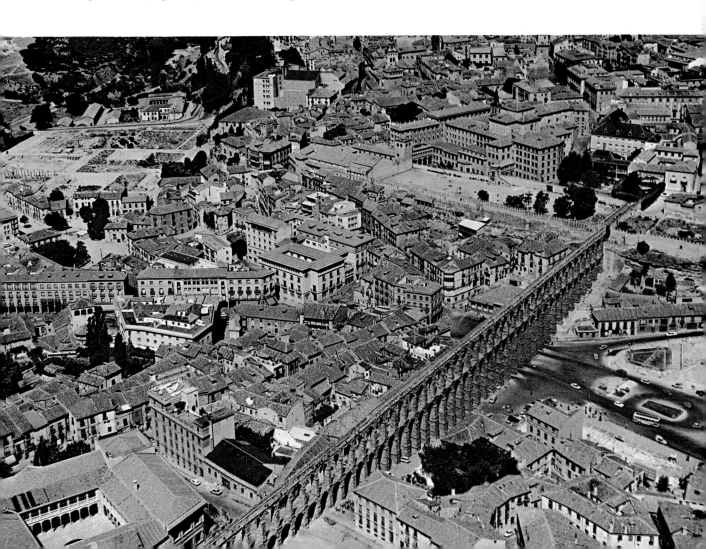

A general view of Segovia.

Later on, the city gradually lost its commercial and industrial potential and became more closed in on itself, developing into the uniquely enchanting city Segovia is today. It was Charles III himself, during whose reign the Academy of Artillery was installed in the Alcázar of Alfonso VI, who engaged the architects Sabatini and Ventura Rodríguez to embellish this unusual city, and make it so unique.

THE CITY WALLS

The mediaeval city walls built in the XI and XII centuries are still preserved with architectural dignity; they have been restored and form a stone girdle round Segovia of some two and a half kilometres in length. Although in certain parts the buildings leaning on the walls almost hide their silhouette, they do give Segovia that special atmosphere which enhances its charm as a city. Three of the seven former city gates are still extant: that of San Andrés — a gateway opening onto the walley of the Eresma with its fine warlike appearance —, the Santiago gateway — also facing the land watered by the Eresma, with its horseshoe archways in mudéjar style — and the San Cebrián gateway, beside which there is a stone cross.

The gates of San Andrés and San Cebrián, two of the seven still preserved in the mediaeval walls which gird the city and give it that distinctive architectural note reminiscent of its ancient and distinguished historical past.

Two fine views of
Segovia where the
outline of the Alcázar
and the Cathedral
can clearly be seen.

A panoramic view of
Segovia with the Roman
aqueduct in the foreground
standing out unmistakably
against its urban
background which stretches
out at either side of the
elegant arches; the city
appears to look at itself
through the arches and to
contemplate with pride its
growth and vitality.

THE AQUEDUCT

One of the most important monuments of antiquity, this aqueduct represents, in Roman architecture, the most successful synthesis of art and technicality. It is situated in the Plazuela del Azoguejo, one of the most typically characteristic places in Segovia, and without any doubt constitutes the most representative element in the city with its majestic presence and inimitable personality. To look at this massive granite monument is to be immediately and profoundly impressed. Any adjective becomes pale and meaningless beside the grandiose architecture of the Aqueduct.

The heraldic symbol of Segovia, the aqueduct brings the waters of the river Acebeda to the city. The archways begin, scarcely emerging from out of the ground, in the east, and adapting themselves to the declivities in the ground, proceed towards the west until they reach the Díaz Sanz Square when they take a sudden turn and form a daring and almost miraculous angle facing the north where the double archway begins, this reaches its maximum height in

the Plaza del Azoguejo. At this point, the deepest in the valley, where the aqueduct is changed into a monumentally graceful triumphal archway, it suddenly, shortly after, goes considerably smaller, until it finally comes to an end in the Plaza del Seminario.

Although the date of its construction is not known with complete certainty some researchers say it was erected between the second half of the first century and the beginning of the second, during the reigns therefore, of the Emperors Vespasian and Trajan.

The aqueduct is 728 metres in length and its maximum height is 28.29 metres. There are altogether 167 archways. From the San Ildefonso road to the Díaz Sanz square there are 75 simple archways, then there are 88 double ones and then another four simple ones. In the first section of the aqueduct there are 36 archways with an ogival curve which are those reconstructed in the XVth century to restore the part destroyed by the Arabs in 1072.

The aqueduct is, for Segovia, a city of monuments par excellence its most important, original and splendid architectural landmark.

The robust and illustrious arches of the arqueduct dominate the city landscape and in this curious photograph cast their imposing shadow over the street which seems completely romanized with both the presence and the reflection of the famous monument.

The majestic presence of the aqueduct
dominates the city from every angle.

ROMA
A
SEGOVIA
EN EL
BIMILENARIO
DE SU
ACUEDUCTO
MCMLXXIV

The prolonged presence of the Roman aqueduct in Segovia (its two thousandth anniversary was in 1974) not only demonstrates the admirable strength of its structure but the markedly Roman personality of the city which is symbolized here in this modern monument erected in honour of the she-wolf of Rome.

The wide Oriente square and the aqueduct make up a harmonious whole which, in this splendid view, becomes a synthesis in Segovia of antiquity, with the ancient Roman architecture and modernity, with the presence of the city and the outline of the hills on the horizon.

A panoramic view of the Cathedral taken from La Piedad.

THE CATHEDRAL

The old cathedral of Santa María, a XII century Romanesque church, was situated where the Alcázar gardens are at the present time and was partly destroyed in 1521 during the rebellion of the "comuneros". Four years later, the task of building a new cathedral was begun; the former convent of las Clarisas and about a hundred more houses were demolished for the cathedral to be built on the highest part of the city.

Although the cathedral was built in the middle of the XVI century when the Renaissance style was already predominant in Spain, its structure is pure Gothic. During the first phase of construction, work was under the direction of Juan Gil de Hontañón and later under García de Cubillas with the collaboration of Rodrigo Gil, who was responsible for the work on the cathedral of Salamanca, Francisco Vázquez and Alonso Martínez. On the death of Cubillas, Rodrigo Gil, the son of Juan Gil de Hontañón, undertook the direction of work on the cathedral of Segovia.

It is, without any doubt one of the finest ogival monuments in Spain and

An impressive close up of the cathedral which, in the words of Ortega y Gasset, "sails among yellow corn" and looks like "an enormous mystical liner hiding the rest of the buildings with its bulk", and they huddle round as if looking to the monument for protection.

A view of the cathedral from el Pinarillo.

has been aptly named, "Lady of Spanish cathedrals". The cathedral over-looks the entire city and from its tower, 88 metres high, there is a vast panoramic view of the surrounding countryside. Consecrated in 1768, the church has a length of 105 metres, is 50 metres wide and 33 metres high in the central nave.

On the outside there are outstanding features— the slim windows, fantastic gargoyles, graceful buttresses and the dome which is one of the most attractive in Spain. The north side is in herrerian style, the portico being of special note. From whichever angle the cathedral is viewed, it presents an impressive architectural sight. The apse, with outjutting hemihexagonal chapels has an admirable harmony of line.

In the inside of the church, the floor in the shape of a latin cross with its three naves separated by pillars with circular bases, and the seven absidal chapels, are of particular note, so too are—the chapel of Saints Cosme and Damian on account of its fine Virgin sculpted by Gregorio Fernández—the chapel of the Conception with its excellent picture gallery and lovely ma-

An evocative view of the cathedral with its lovely silhouette outlined against the blue of the Segovian night; the edging of its filigreed stonework looks like lace made by a delicate and sensitive hand.

The rear part of the cathedral.

hogany screen, the chapel of La Piedad, enclosed by a valuable plateresque grille where a magnificent altar-piece is kept—the work of Juan de Juni—and a triptych painted by Ambrosius Benson, the chapel of Saint Barbara with its baptismal font donated by Henry IV, and the Sagrarium chapel with a superb figure of Christ sculpted by Pereira on a curious ceramic altar made by Daniel de Zuloaga. The stained glass windows and the two cathedral organs are also of interest.

The Museum and the Chapter House merit a description of their own. The former houses some important pictures atributed to Van Eyck, Morales, Berruguete and other famous painters, a XIII century statue of the Virgin, a reliquary attributed to Benvenuto Cellini, the carriage which takes part in the Corpus Christi procession, old royal documents, ancient coins, and one of the most valuable collections of incunabulars in Spain. The Chapter House with its artistic wainscoting, possesses apart from the tomb of the legendary jewess, María del Salto, placed in the outside wall of the cloister, an impressive painting by Valdés Leal and another by Esquivel of enormous dimensions, together with a fine collection of Gobelins tapestries.

The pulpit and rail in front of the high altar of the cathedral whose chapel was begun to be built in the year 1563 at the same time as the retro-choir and the apse, under the direction of Rodrigo Gil de Hontañón and according to the plans made by his father, Juan Gil de Hontañón already deceased.

The cathedral nave with the "Burial of Christ" in the Chapel de la Piedad, and a XVI century triptych.

A carriage-monstrance belonging to the cathedral treasure.

A triptych by Benson dating from the XVI century and the Brussels tapestery room.

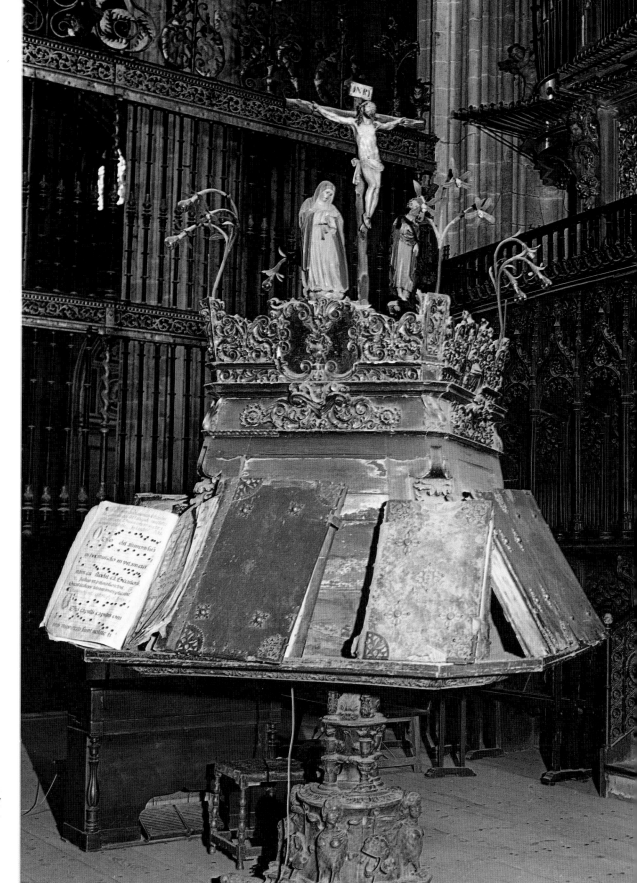

*The Vasco
Lectern situated
in the choir
of the cathedral.*

*A view of the
main square
with the
cathedral in the
background.*

THE CHURCH OF SAINT MICHAEL

The former Romanesque church where Isabella the Catholic was crowned on December 13th 1474, collapsed in 1532. The present church was built in 1558. Its wide Gothic nave and the reredos on the high altar are of interest as well as the tombs, a Gothic chalice with an enamelled coat of arms and a valuable processional cross made by Diego Muñoz. The church of Saint Michael is in the Plaza Mayor.

THE TOWN HALL

The town hall is in a building in the Plaza Mayor, built by Pedro de Brizuela in the XVII century according to the maxims of Renaissance aesthetics. In side the building is the "white room" with decoration in Elizabethan style, a valuable triptych by Benson and pictures signed by Madrazo and other painters.

The front of the Town Hall. ▷

A close-up of the main square and the cathedral.

The Town Hall
conference
chamber.

The white
chamber in the
Town Hall.

THE ALCAZAR

Perched on a rocky spur rising above the confluence of the Eresma and the Clamores where is overlooks all the passes into the valley, the Alcázar affords us the most genuine picture of a Spanish castle. From its high position Segovia and all the surrounding countryside can be clearly seen, the Alcázar itself forming an integral part of that countryside.

Although it is not known when it was founded, there apparently existed a fortress there during the time of the Roman domination which was later used by the Moslems. But it was Alfonso VI who, after the reconquest, first began to initiate extensions in the Alcázar, where doña Berenguela, the mother of Saint Ferdinand, was born. This bastion of Segovia was constantly involved in historical events. In the year 1256, while the Cortes of don Alfonso the Wise were meeting in the Alcázar, part of the building collapsed but was reconstructed later on. Other monarchs connected with the Alcázar were Sancho IV, Ferdinand IV, Alfonso XI, don Pedro the Cruel – who took refuge in Segovia after his flight from Toro–, John I who summoned

A poetic view of the Alcázar with the river Eresma in the foreground.

An aerial view of the famous Alcázar at Segovia.

An original night time view of the Alcázar whose unmistakable outline stands out like a ship sailing through the sea in the darkness.

A fine close up of the Alcázar in relief against the blue sky; "its beautiful walls" according to the writer Eugenio Noel, " say many things to the soul" and "enchant it like a fairy tale".

A close up of the Patio del Reloj, one of the most characteristic parts of the Alcázar which has succeeded in keeping the purity of its original design.

The reknowned outlines of the Alcázar and the Cathedral make an harmonious picture and lend Segovia an air of antiquity in which the passage of time has left behind its charming historical and artistic imprint.

A charming view of the Alcázar at Segovia with its impressive group of seven towers among which the most outstandingly beautiful is that of Juan II; its cornises are surrounded with high dies and are adorned with a series of spheres and filigreed mouldings reaching up into the sky and glimpsed through elegant windowns.

This photograph shows to effect the richness of the stained glass windows in the Alcázar with their markedly mediaeval subjects.

A view of the so-called "King's bedroom" where there are two Moorish doors, copies of those in the former palace of Enrique IV donated by the Count of Almodóvar.

The sumptuous Throne Room with its fine Moorish frieze and XV century panelling.

the Cortes Generales in Segovia on three occasions, Henry III, who lived in the castle, and John II and Henry IV who made important contributions to the splendour of the fortress. Furthermore, the Catholic Kings, Charles I, Philip II, Philip III and Charles III — who set up the artillery academy in the castle, visited and on more than one occasion took on responsabilities regarding the castle.

The last piece of restoration was carried out in 1940, and the Alcázar has now recouped all its past grandeur and architectural splendour. At the present time the Alcázar is converted into a military archive and is a most interesting and evocative place to visit; one's imagination can wander back through the building's historical past and at the same time many interesting things can be seen — the original Torre del Homenaje, the Juan II tower, the elegant Sala de la Galera, the "executioner's corridor", the dark dungeons, the Romanesque grille giving access to the Treasure Chamber and the courtyard built by Diego de Matienzo in the XVIth century. In short, here is a complete world of fantasy and reality, of history and legend.

*The spacious Sala de la Galera still
conserves its original sober aristocratic
elegance.*

That much travelled writer Eugenio Noel was impressed and captivated
by the Alcázar, which, he said, appears, and "soon remains alone in our
field of vision, its lovely silhouette filling the horizon. Seated on a large
rock in the gigantic cave, I think about old Segovia and that Alcázar. Its
rib cut like the prow of a boat, the rock elevates the castle to unbelieved
heights with an untamed majesty... It is a castle that does not cause fear
or offence. It fascinates, captivates and attracts...".

*A view of the Armoury
in the Alcázar.*

*One of the murals
decorating the interior
of the Alcázar.*

*The original
façade of the
Casa de los Pico*

THE CITY

Its illustrious historical past and great wealth of monuments scattered throughout the length and breadth of Segovia for many centuries has made it an unforgettable place with a very personal attraction. The essence of its personality is captured in these lines by Dionisio Ridruejo:

Entre arboledas la pesada quilla
y hacia el llano sin sombra aventurada
desgajas de la sierra, ágil, dorada,
la tenue primavera de Castilla.

Nave de soledad, alta, arbolada
de dulce otoño cuando el sol se humilla
mientras llegan triunfantes a tu orilla
los arcos de la sed petrificada.

Oigo mi tiempo en el Eresma frío
que lame tu reflejo con tus horas
y en la ribera espadas y ganados.

Y te enalteces más y con más brío
sobre árboles y peñas mientras lloras
verdor entre tus muros quebrantados.

A fine close up of the atrium of San Martín, from whose enchanting archways one can see the bustle of the street; in the background against the blue of the sky is the artistic shape of the Cathedral.

Segovia has· views of surprising beauty from a great variety of angles and never loses any of its uniqueness. However or from wherever you look at it, it is still unmistakably Segovia. Its fascinating light is a sort of miracle produced by the proximity of city with country. "The light — writes the marquis of Lozoya — turns an afternoon in Segovia, especially in the last months of summer and the first months of autumn, into an unforgettable celebration. During the minutes before sunset, the city seems all alight. Sometimes, the towers stand out against slate-grey clouds. It is then, as Lucas Dubreton noted in his fine book "Le roi sauvage", when the towers of Segovia have an inner light which goes on shining when everything around them has gone out."

It is difficult to choose routes in Segovia. You have to see everything. Gaze at each and every one of its changing views, drink in its spiritual meaning

A view of the Torreón de los Lozoyas.

The monument to Juan Bravo.

The house of the Marquis of Moya. ▷

The Romanesque façade of the palace of the Marquis of Lozoya. ▷

The façade of the Palacio de Quintanar. ▷

The Torreón Arias-Dávila. ▷

The Caja de Ahorros y Monte de Piedad de Segovia (Building Society) occupies a magnificent building in modern style whose architecture mingles intelligently with the general tone of the city.

and let your impressions wander free. It is the sort of city which is impossible to force into a methodically thought out tourist trip. Segovia is a mystery to be unravelled at leisure without haste and with a pre-disposition to be surprised at every moment.

If you do it like this, you will live through moments of intense beauty — contemplating the Plaza Mayor in all its noble sweep, getting lost in the intricate and evocative Juderías, admiring the aristocratic façades of the segovian palaces — the palace of the Marquis of Quintanar, of the Tordesillas, the Marquis of Lozoya, of Maldonado..., the plazuela del Azoguejo, the district of San Esteban, and of las Canonjías, the Clamores area, or wandering through the orchands and poplar groves which decorate the valley of the Eresma. In addition to all the scenic delights, Segovia has a noble character, its people are cordial and sober, their speech precise and concise and the women are deliciously feminine, and lovely.

Several views of the differing aspects of Segovia showing the complete symbiosis between the old and the new elements in the city.

THE SAN QUIRCE ACADEMY OF HISTORY AND ART

This former church of San Quirce became the seat of the popular university of Segovia in 1927. At the present time it is used by Academy of History and Art which depends on the Council for Scientific Research.

THE PROVINCIAL MUSEUM

This is to be found in the so-called "House of the nobleman" in the Calle de San Agustín, and houses some interesting collections of paintings, sculpture and engravings. Among the things inherited by the museum are some tablets of Hispano-Flemish painting, and several engravings by Durero and Rembrant.

The Gothic chapel which was formerly the Old People's Hospital situated beside the plaza de San Martín depends on the Provincial Museum where an interesting collection of prehistoric and Visigothic remains from the necropolis of the province of Segovia can be seen.

"The Descent", a XV century work by the cleric Contreras painted on wood, which together with the triptych the "Maestro de las clavellinas" and "The adoration of the Kings" of the Berruguete school, is one of the best pieces in the Provincial Museum.

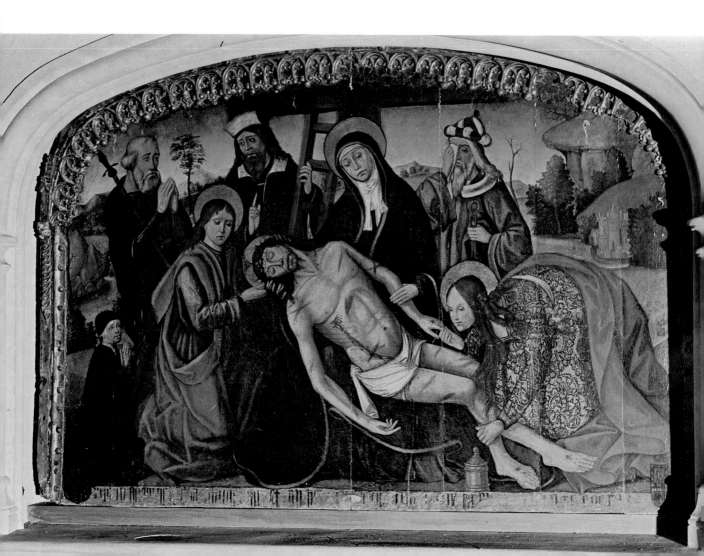

This exquisite relief in the Provincial Museum belongs to the Santa Columba altar-piece and is a magnificent XVI century polychrome whose figures have been worked with outstanding ability showing a classic popular and religious motif of charming spontaneity.

A typical street in the Judería Nueva.

A fine view of the attractive calle de los Desamparados.

THE CONVENT OF CORPUS CHRISTI

This is the former synagogue, built in the XIIIth century whose style is reminiscent of that of Santa María la Blanca in Toledo. Here, a famous jewish sacrilege took place in 1410 and it afterwards became consecrated as a Catholic church. It is situated in the square of the same name and after being burnt down in 1889, was reconstructed, conserving up to the present time, parts of the former Gothic structure, some archways, and the stretch of wall which alludes to the story of the sacrilege or "miracle of the synagogue".

THE HOUSE OF ANTONIO MACHADO

This is situated in the steep and narrow Calle de los Desamparados in the San Esteban quarter. It is not far from the San Juan de Dios convent and is a small house of modest appearance; there is a stone bust of the great poet

Antonio Machado in the courtyard. The author of "Campos de Castilla" lived in this house for twelve years and it was probably here where he wrote the poem entitled "The Miracle", which begins with the following lines:

One afternoon
In Segovia
Walking through the poplar grove
Bathed by the Eresma
To read my Bible,
I reached for my glasses-case,
Searching for this scaffolding of my sight,
This jutting balcony to my eyes.

THE DANIEL ZULOAGA MUSEUM

The museum is in the former church of San Juan de los Caballeros, it is a XII century Romanesque structure built beside the Plaza de Colmenares; at the same time it is the home of the School of Ceramic Art. The ceramic artist Daniel Zuloaga established his studio in this old church in 1905. At the present time it houses an interesting collection of pieces of ceramic made by the artist himself together with several paintings by Ignacio Zuloaga.

A view of one of the rooms in the Zuloaga Museum which has a fine collection of pottery and several pieces of sculpture, pictures, furniture and objects collected by the artist who created and gave his name to this interesting Segovian museum.

THE HISTORICAL ARCHIVE

The archives occupy the former Royal Prison in the Calle de Juan Bravo. It was here where the famous Spanish dramatist Lope de Vega was detained in 1577. In the archives there is an important collection of documents of a historical nature relating to Segovia. The entrance to the building is of interest – a work by Pedro de Brizuela – and so too is another Romanesque door situated in one of the exhibition rooms.

THE CHURCH OF SAINT MARTIN

This church is in the calle de Juan Bravo, and overlooks a fine cityscape which includes the squares of Saint Martin and Medina del Campo. It is an example of pure Romanesque style and was built in the XII century. Its beautiful atria and fine portals are especially noteworthy, as are its apses, one of which has been discovered only recently, and the tower. In the interior is the tomb of the Herrera family, with its valuable reredos, a recumbent figure of Christ by Gregorio Fernández, a statue of Saint Francis of Assisi – an original work by Pedro de Mena – and a flemish triptych.

The main façade and detail from the church of San Martín, one of the loveliest Romanesque churches in Segovia; inside are kept some valuable art treasures, especially pieces of sculpture and paintings.

*A view of the
Plaza de las
Sirenas with
the church of
San Martín.*

THE CHURCH OF SAINT STEPHEN

Built in transitional Romanesque style, it is located in the irregularly shaped but attractive little Saint Stephen's square. The most interesting feature of this church is its slender tower—known as the "queen of Spanish towers"—. It is made up of five parts and is 53 metres high; in 1896 it was declared a National Monument. The atrium has also conserved the purity of its original style.

THE CHURCH OF THE TRINITY

This is a XIIth century Romanesque church sited on the charming square of the same name. On the main door is the labarum, with alpha and omega engraved on it. Of interest is the artistic arcade, discovered some twenty years ago. Also worthy of mention are the graceful atrium, the adjoining Gothic chapel, and the Holy Visage, a magnificent painting by Ambrosius Benson.

THE PARISH OF SAINT NICHOLAS

A Romanesque church of the XIIth century, situated in the square of the same name. It has interesting apses and a tower. On restoring it some years ago an interesting XIVth century tomb was found in one of the apses containing the mummified body of a knight.

An outstanding close-up of the Romanesque church of San Esteban.

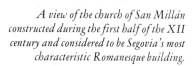
A view of the church of San Millán constructed during the first half of the XII century and considered to be Segovia's most characteristic Romanesque building.

The graceful arches of the church of San Millán open in harmony and with singular Romanesque elegance onto the streets of the city immutably contemplating its modern structure.

THE CHURCH OF SAINT LAURENCE

Dominating the area of the same name, the church is in a lovely valley bathed by the waters of the river Eresma. It is XII century Romanesque in style and has three splendid apses, a fine atrium and a charming tower built, not in stone but in brick, which is unique in all Segovia. Inside the church there is an original triptych by Benito Giralte and Rodrigo de Segovia.

THE CONVENT OF THE BAREFOOT CARMELITES

In the same place where Saint John de la Mata founded a convent of Trinitarians in 1206, right in the valley of the Eresma, there arose, twelve years later, another convent founded by Saint John of the Cross with the help of doña Ana de Peñalosa. The church, built on top of the previous one at the beginning of the XVII century has a cross and dome. Shortly afterwards the chapel was built where, since October 11th 1927, lie the remains, in a profusely adorned urn, of Saint John of the Cross, the highest exponent of Spanish mystic poetry. In the lovely spacious orchard of the convent, above the so-called "Peñas Grajeras" there is a hermitage near a cave where the carmelite saint used to retire to pray, and beside this, a cypress tree planted by his own hand.

Detail from the church of San Millán showing the extraordinary rich adornments in this fine Romanesque church.

The fine chaffron which tops the brick tower on the church of San Lorenzo forms a harmonious group with the Romanesque apses on the church itself, one of the most original buildings in the city.

THE SANCTUARY OF LA FUENCISLA

This sanctuary is surrounded by particularly beautiful countryside and is sheltered by great cliffs not far from the confluence of the rivers Clamores and Eresma. It is a very popular place with segovians and is dedicated to Our Lady de la Fuencisla, Patroness and Mediator of the city. Built in 1598 and 1613, the sanctury is constructed in the shape of a greek cross mounted on a square. There is a magnificent altar piece by Pedro de la Torre and Yosef Rodes, a valuable gilded screen in the presbitry and an iron pulpit in the best Gothic style donated by Juan de Monreal.

The Virgin de Fuencisla, according to popular legend, was found in the now non-existent parish of San Gil where it had been hidden from the Arabs; the statue of the Virgin saved the life of a jewish girl who had been unjustly condemned to be flung over a precipice. When the young girl exclaimed "Help me Christian Virgin", Our Lady of Fuencisla held her in the air and let her gently down onto the ground. The young jewess, being saved, was converted to Christianity and changed her name from Esther to María, after that becoming popularly known as María del Salto.

Views of the interior and exterior of the charming archway in the Sanctuary of La Fuencisla, situated in one of the loveliest beauty spots in Segovia where many go to celebrate the feast of the Virgin-Patroness of the city.

A statue of Our Lady de la Fuencisla, the patroness of Segovia.

A view of the church of Veracruz or los Templarios.

THE CHURCH OF VERACRUZ

This is also called the church of the Templars and is beside the road to Zamarramal in the district of San Marcos. Founded by the Knights Templar, it was consecrated in 1208 and still conserves a relic of the Holy Cross donated by Honorius III in 1226 which gave the church its name. Built on Romanesque lines, it consists of a poligonal base with two storeys and a surrounding nave. Under the dome on the second floor is the central stone (decorated with interlaced horseshoe archways) before which the novice knights kept vigil over their arms. The church of Veracruz was declared a National Monument in 1919.

THE CONVENT OF THE HOLY CROSS

Situated at the foot of the city wall, not far from the district of Saint Lorenzo, in the middle of the Eresma valley, this convent was abandoned in the XIXth century and has been given over to the Provincial Charitable Organization. The church was built it 1218 by Saint Domingo above a grotto in which he had sought refuge. Reconstructed in the XVth century, it has a beautiful plateresque portal with kneeling statues of the Catholic kings Ferdinand and Isabella, a fine Gothic ceiling and an excellent sculpture of Saint Martin.

The plateresque style portal of the church of Santa Cruz la Real built in the XV century and of the school of Juan Guas; a former holiday palace of Enrique IV and later on a Franciscan convent.

The tower and chaffron belonging to the church of San Justo beside the graceful Romanesque apse of the church built in the XII century, where not long ago some splendid mural paintings were discovered.

THE MONASTERY OF EL PARRAL

The church and monastery of el Parral are surrounded by shady groves of poplar trees near the river Eresma. The area, extending from the San Lorenzo district to Saint Mark's is of an extraordinary beauty and fully justifies the popular segovian rhyme: "De los huertos al Parral, paraíso terrenal". (From the orchards to el Parral — earthly paradise).

According to tradition, this monastery belonging to the Hieronymite monks was founded by don Juan Pacheco, the first Marquis of Villena, after escaping from a serious quarrel he had at that time by invoking the Virgins's intercession. This episode is alluded to on a stone set into the wall leading to the monastery.

Apparently, building on the convent was begun in 1455, during the reign of Henry IV. It is in mudéjar Gothic style and slightly reminiscent of the monastery of Guadalupe. The church is of a purer Gothic style and work on it was carried out by Juan Gallego, Bonifacio Guas, and Pedro Polido. The plateresque tower, belonging to the XVI century is the work of Juan

The façade of the Parral Monastery appearing, under the tower of Lastrilla, "close to the river, in a deep gorge full of dense trees with thick foliage", as Pío Baroja saw it, dominating the Castilian countryside with its vigorous personality.

The high altar in the monastery of El Parral.

Campero. Declared a National Monument in 1914, many different and valuable works of art to be found in el Parral, the most outstanding of these being: the reredos on the high altar, in plateresque style, the work of painter Francisco González; the two tombs on either side, with the praying figures of Juan Pacheco and his wife doña María Portocarrero; the tomb situated on the arms of the cross, of doña Beatriz Pacheco, countess of Medellín, in Gothic style, and the twelve statues of the apostles which flank the windows of the church together with the coats of arms ot the Pachecos.

A view of part of the lovely cloister in the El Parral monastery.

Inside doorway leading to the high altar in the El Parral monastery.

An evocative shot of the cloister in the El Parral monastery.

THE CONVENT OF SAINT ANTHONY THE ROYAL

Founded by Henry IV towards the middle of the XV century and originally designed as a princely residence, it is located in the area formerly known as "El Campillo", on the spit of land joining the highest part of the city to the plateau. At the present time it is a cloistered convent. The church, Gothic with mudejar additions, has a beautiful portal and artistic moorish panelling. The cloister, pulpit, Chapter House, three Flemish triptychs, and a splendid Calvary called "de Bruselas" are especially noteworthy.

This building was donated by Enrique IV to the Franciscan Observers. When, in 1488, the monks occupying it moved to the Convent of San Francisco, the present seat of the Artillery Academy, the Santa Clara nuns occupied San Antonio el Real where they have remained to this day. Not far from this convent is that of Saint Isabel, in Gothic style, built in the XV century.

The chamber of the Kings —the sacristy— in the Convent of San Antonio.

A close up of the façade of the Convent of San Antonio el Real, a former royal residence now occupied by cloistered Clare nuns.

This photograph brings out the extraordinary plasticity of this Flemish Calvary, dated XV century and called "de Bruselas"; it is one of the most valuable pieces in the Convent of San Antonio el Real.

A view of the chapter house in the Convent of San Antonio.

A room which gives an idea of the riches contained in the Convent of San Antonio.

Cándido, the Mesonero
Mayor of Castile,
officiating in the appetising
gastronomic ritual of
the roasting of the sucking
pig.

A view of one of the
rooms in the famous Mesón
de Cándido

GASTRONOMY

The two basic dishes of Segovia—a city where it is possible to eat as of yore—are lamb and roast sucking pig. Both dishes are well cooked in this region and can be recommended to anyone, both the gourmet and the gourmand. When mentioning roasts, it is impossibble not to include the Meson de Candido and its owner who has justifiably been awarded the honourable title of Mesonero Mayor de Castilla; in this restaurant the lamb and sucking pig are the most memorable dishes. The aforementioned restaurant is famous gastronomically not only in Spain but abroad. The house was built in the XV century and the Meson (or inn) has been operating as it does today since 1860.

Other typically segovian dishes are, garlick soup with pork and ham, a lamb stew, meat stew, stew with meat balls, cod cooked with garlick, fried trout or trout in escabeche, which, according to the marquis of Lozoya "were sampled by the Prince of Wales, who became Charles I, during his romantic journey to Spain, in the XVII century", river crabs and frogs legs are also available and there are excellent sausages made in Cantimpalos and Bernuy de Porreros.

Desserts in Segovia are many and varied. The most outstanding are the "yemas", the "bizcocho", and the "segovian punch".

To take with these succulent dishes there is a very high grade local wine.

The dining room of the Segovian restaurant known as "La Taurina" whose decoration is a faithful reflection of the typical Castilian style.

Juanito, the popular Master of the Roasts of the restaurant "La Taurina", standing before tables laden with appetising Segovian dishes among which the most outstanding are the incomparable roasts, and specially the typical sucking pig, a dish capable of giving an appetite to the most indifferent of mortals.

Roast sucking pig in the "Mesón del Duque". The roasting is an operation performed according to the most orthodox rituals of Castilian cookery.

A view of the mediaeval Segovian dining-room in the "Mesón del Duque" decorated in typically Castilian style with the sober and the picturesque existing in complete harmony.

A roasting oven in the typical "Mesón del Duque" with some succulent meats.

Two children in typical Segovian costume in front of the beautiful courtyard of the church of St. Martin, one of the most attractive Romanesque monuments in the city.

THE FOLKLORE OF SEGOVIA

Segovia and its province possess some rich and attractive folklore. The annual festivities in the capital are celebrated in honour of Saint John and Saint Peter between the 24th and 29th of June. These are animated and brilliant festivities with accompanying religious services, dancing or different types and bull fights. The Día de Segovia is also an important day held on the first Sunday in July. Many people from the outlying provinces come to the capital on that day, and an excursion is organized to La Granja. The most traditional festivity is that of the patron San Frutos held on the 25th of October.

Another popular fiesta is Santa Agueda's day which is celebrated in the village of Zamarramala, at a distance of 3 kilometres from Segovia. On that day a woman takes command in the village for the whole day. Dressed as a mayoress — with a skirt or cape in blue or claret colour with silver stripes and velvet fringes, a velvet skirt and a fine linen shirt —, the elected lady presides over a series of religious ceremonies.

The popular festivities in Cuéllar, Pedraza, Sepúlveda, Turégano, Riaza, "de la Soterraña" in Santa María de Nieva and la Fuencisla on the last Sunday in September are also of note.

The traditional segovian songs usually allude to old romances. Lullabyes are also deeply rooted in segovian folklore. The most popular dances are accompanied by typical "paloteos". The dancers — danzantes — interrupt the dance from time to time to make "paloteo", that is to clash the "palotes" each one carries in his hand.

There are two popular types of house in the province of Segovia: that of the plains and the mountain type. In the first type, the most important rooms are the entrance and the kitchen. In the mountain house, generally made of masonry bound with mud with only one storey and few windows, the most important rooms are the entrance, the kitchen, the yard and the stable.

A youthful pair showing off typical Segovian dress with the Alcázar in the background watching the children in a lordly fashion from its pointed towers. A picturesque composition with people, art, and history united in a happy synthesis.

The "La Fama" garden in the Granja de San Ildefonso with age-old trees in the foreground offering their cool shade to the visitor and the splendid palace in the background where valuable collections of tapestries, antique furniture, pictures and other priceless objects are kept.

(Reproduction authorized by the National Patrimony).

LA GRANJA DE SAN ILDEFONSO

The town of San Ildefonso is 11 kilometres from Segovia in the foothills of the Guadarrama mountains. A top class summer resort, it is at a height of 1,190 metres above sea level. Its origin dates from the year 1450 when Henry IV had a hermitage built and dedicated it to San Ildefonso along with a house in the beautiful spot then called Casar del Pollo, situated in the midst of leafy woods where the sovereigns of Castile used to go hunting. Later on the hermitage was given by the Catholic Kings to the Hieronymite monks of El Parral who rebuilt the house, surrounding it with orchards and gardens and installing a farm there for rest and convalescence. Such is the origin, then, of the San Ildefonso farm, which is so famous today.

Towards the middle of the XVIII century, Philip V came upon the hermita-

ge while out hunting and was so enchanted with the beauty of the place that he decided to build gardens similar to those at Versailles in that spot. Work was begun in 1721 according to plans drawn up by Teodoro Ardemans. At the same time, Carlier, the sculptor and the gardener Bontelou were in charge of the laying out and building of the famous gardens surrounding the palace. Two years later the palace was blessed and its church consecrated. The palace is in the shape of an elongated rectangle, the main façade measuring 155 metres in length by 13 high, and the side walls, built later, are 45 metres long. The main façade has a graceful portal with four caryatids above it simbolizing the seasons of the year. The church, in the rear portion of the palace is in the shape of a latin cross with a fine dome. Before it caught fire in 1918, it was beautifully decorated by Bayeu and Maella.

A view of the sumptuous Throne Room in the San Ildefonso Palace showing the rich furnishings including the splendid giant lamps, fine polychromed tapestries and carpets and ceiling paintings.

(Reproduction authorized by the National Patrimony).

A close up of the fountain of the Baths of Diana, one of the loveliest in the gardens surrounding the palace of San Ildefonso which for their beauty and vastness have been compared to those at Versailles.

On the left of the high altar is a mausoleum containing the remains of Philip V and Isabel de Farnese.

The palace is now a museum and some of the best tapestries in Europe can be seen in its rooms along with interesting furniture of the time, magnificent lamps and valuable paintings.

There are 145 hectares of magnificent gardens surrounding the palace. They are set out with the elegance dictated by Le Nôtre in his plans for those at Versailles. Many lovely munumental fountains with artistic statues by Fremin, Pitue, Dumandre and Thierry, decorate the immense green precinct composed of the gardens, the wood — where there are more than 10,000

trees of the most varied and exotic types –, the maze and the artificial lake called "The Sea". The most outstanding of the fountains receiving their water from "The Sea" are "La Fama" with its fantastic jet of water reaching 47 metres in height, "Los baños de Diana" – with a statue of the godess surrounded by twenty nymphs –, "las Ranas" (the frogs) "Las tres gracias" (the three graces), "Anfititre", "Apolo", "El Canastillo" and "La Gran Cascada" opposite the main façade of the palace. Contemplated as a whole-palace, gardens, wood and lake, with the filigreed playing of 140 fountains, have the appearance of a romantic dream place from the "Thousand and one nights".

A magnificent view of the Palace garden with the Fountain of Anfitrite in the foreground, flanked by thick-topped trees and with the sturdy Segovian mountains as an impressive back drop, their primaeval bulk contrasting markedly with the neatly cut lawns in the gardens.

(Reproduction authorized by the National Patrimony).

THE PALACE OF RIOFRIO

Sited in the middle of a vast thick wood of cork oaks, some 12 kilometres from San Ildefonso is the palace of Riofrío. "Taking the road from Madrid to Segovia — writes the great traveller and writer, Alvaro Ruibal — leaving the gloomy stony tracts of El Pinar, on the hill to the left can be seen the palace of Riofrío. A building broader than tall with rose coloured stone facings and green windows, emerging from its brief height surrounded by a sparse wood of cork oaks... How is such a miracle possible? How can such a luxurious italian palace arise from this untamed countryside? Alvaro Ruibal is quite

right: it is in effect a true miracle defying logic and ecology. The palace was buit in the XVIII century at the order of Isabel de Farnese and work was finished during the reign of Charles III. It is a spacious square building, in neoclassic style, surrounded by a wood of some 700 hectares in whose density live great quantities of deer, buck, and many other species providing game for the memorable royal hunts which took place throughout the reigns of Alfonso XII and Alfonso XIII.

The palace has a magnificent courtyard and a regal main staircase and offers the visitor room upon room full of valuable works of art, tapestries antique furniture and paintings. Of late it has been converted into the Museum of hunting.

Riofrío is some 10 km. from Segovia and without doubt one of the most impressive beauty spots in the province. There is no guide better than the marquis of Lozoya for a journey along the routes of Segovia. Let us then go with him to Riofrío. "After crossing the Guadarrama road" writes the marquis, "the way goes through the Revenga woods, in which a Roma-nesque hermitage can be seen hidden in the foliage. The woods with the largest quantity of storks in the locality reach the walls of the Riofrío estate, and the guards kindly opened the gate". The Riofrío palace "is the most Roman" of all the Spanish palaces and the pleasant rose-coloured tint of the plastering contributes to this romanism. As in the Royal Palace at Madrid, every façade has a central portion flanked by others jutting out slightly. The flying balconies on the main floor have dust-guards over their lintels in alternately triangular or semi-circular shapes. The building is topped by a balustrade interrupted in sections by plinths with vases of flowers sculpted in limestone by Bartolomé Sexmini". A visit to Riofrío will leave an unforgettable memory in the mind of the person who goes there.

A view of the room in the Charles V Hunting Lodge where beside several hunting motifs is a full length portrait of the Emperor.

An angle of the main staircase of the palace at Riofrío taken from the entrance.

VILLACASTIN

This town has a marked personality, its streets houses flanked by interesting houses and its fine church a mixture of Gothic and escorial styles. There are several important works of Alonso de Herrera to be admired inside the church.

"The houses of Villacastín", says Ramón Carnicer in his book entitled "Fortunes and misfortunes of old Castile", "are solid, made of good stone, hewn from enormous pellets of granite strewn round about. Some are decorated with coats of Arms and on one of them one reads: "I am from Pedro Zúñiga", bearing witness to the former Basque presence in these lands". This is a Castilian village of considerable agricultural importance.

A typical corner of Villacastín.

MARTIN MUÑOZ DE LAS POSADAS

In this interesting town is the magnificent palace of Cardinal don Diego de Espinosa, who was president of Castile in the time of Philip II. There are some important works of art in the church: a "Calvary" apparently painted by El Greco, and the tomb of Cardinal Espinosa, carved in alabaster by Pompeo Leoni.

SANTA MARIA DE NIEVA

This town was founded at the end of the XIV century and its most interesting monument is the Gothic church belonging to the Dominican convent built by Catherine of Lancaster in honour of the Virgin called "La Soterraña". The church has an artistic cloister in transitional Romanesque style which is considered the best in the province, also a valuable altar piece in the Chapel of Saint Jerónimo, with fine sculptures attributed to Berruguete.

The capitals and the cloister in Santa María la Real de Nieva.

The main façade of Santa María la Real de Nieva.

NAVA DE LA ASUNCION

This is one of most progressive towns in Segovia. It is completely surrounded by pine woods and its industrial impetus has led to the exploitation of ist extraordinary abundance of wood.

COCA

This is a historic town, already of some importance in pre-Roman times; known as Cauca in celtiberian times, it was the birthplace of the Emperor Theodosius in the IVth century. There are many interesting monuments in Coca, all overlooked by the moorish castle built at the confluence of the Eresma and Voltoya rivers; the surrounding countryside is of singular beauty. Of interest are the remains of the town walls especially the gate in mudéjar style, the Gothic church of Santa María with the tombs of the Fonseca family, the lords of Coca, and the tower of Saint Nicholas.

Coca still conserves interesting remains of its pre-Roman past, among these are the wild boar sculpted in granite by the Celts.

A fine close up of the Moorish castle of Coca which, according to the marquis of Lozoya, "although it lost in the XIX century its fantastic palacial decoration is one of the loveliest in Spain and is without any doubt the master-piece of Moorish stone masons who are very talented in the use of bricks."

The filigreed outline of the
castle at Coca stands out as
an exotic brick construction
against the sun of Castile.

The castle at Coca rises up
in the middle of a beautiful
spot bathed by the waters of
the Eresma and the
Voltoya.

CUELLAR

This is the most densely populated town in the province after Segovia itself and is also one of the loveliest. Ist history dates from pre-Roman times and there exist numerous relics of its former splendour. Its most outstanding monument is the Gothic castle, built in the XV century belonging to the Duke of Albuquerque and used as a prison until quite recently. It underwent reconstruction on several occasions and Renaissance and mudejar traces can be found on its predominantly Gothic structure. Its warlike aspect is enhanced by the dies and barbicans on the outside. The spacious courtyard has some interesting arcades in Greco-Roman style. Espronceda, the famous XIX century romantic poet was a prisoner in the castle of Cuéllar.

Other places of interest in the town are the Romanesque apses of the churches of Saint Martin, Saint Andrew and Saint Stephen, the remains of the ancient wall, the convent of Saint Francis, restored by Beltrán de la Cueva, the hospital and the house known as "de la Torre".

FUENTIDUEÑA

This town was, on several occasions, the royal residence of Alfonso VIII and is the complete mediaeval town with its XII century walls surrounding it. Its glorious past is brought back when we examine the ruins of the church of Saint Martin whose splendid Romanesque apse is in a New York museum at the present time. The church of Saint Michael is also interesting.

SEPULVEDA

Some 67 kilometres from the capital of the province, the important village of Sepúlveda rises up from a great rock surrounded by the rivers Caslilla and Duratón. Formerly known as Septempublica, it is rich in monuments; parts of the old city walls are still extant and part of the gate and remains of the old castle; the castle lends the village a romantic air. Other important monuments in Sepúlveda are the Romanesque church of el Salvador which overlooks the village, the church of Santa María de la Peña in the same style, the latter being the patroness of the village. The entire village, called in former times "the village of the seven gates" is a fine monument in itself, with golden coloured stone and curious surrounding countryside scarred with rivers and gorges.

Sepúlveda was reconquered in the X century by count Fernán González and immediately went over to the side of the Catholic Kings.

A general view of Sepúlveda, "whose position", in the opinion of the marquis of Lozoya, "is only rivalled by that of Segovia in Castile"; it has an extraordinarily fine panoramic view.

A view of the castle at Castilnovo. ▷

The church at Riaza. ▷

The church at Ayllón. ▷

A shot of a typical square in Ayllón

Two typical corners of Sepúlveda
with a view of the surrounding
countryside.

CASTILNOVO

At a distance of 8 kilometres from Sepúlveda is the famous castle of Castilnovo. It is a XV century fortress surrounded by bushes and meadows and belonged to don Alvaro de Luna, the marquis of Villena and the Princes Hohenzollern; at the present time it is owned by the Marquis of Quintanar. It has always been lived in and its rooms are sumptuously decorated.

MADERUELO

Lying beside the river Riaza, Maderuelo, an ancient fortified town, still retains traces of its past splendour. The hermitage of the Templars and the parish church are of note.

RIAZA

This is a typical mountain town whose native structure contrasts harmoniously with its modern buildings which have been intelligently integrated into the surrounding countryside. Riaza has an interesting Renaissance church and has been able to conserve its historical personality without renouncing the advantages of industrialization. Another attraction the town has is the delicate-flavoured trout in its streams and the quantity of big game in the nearby mountains.

The popular Sanctuary of the Virgin of Hontanares is quite near and of interest.

AYLLON

Formerly the domain of don Alvaro de Luna, its streets still have that special charm of the mediaeval village. Outstanding among its monuments are the remains of the walls, the castle, and convent founded by Saint Francis of Assisi. The fine Gothic façade of the palace built in the XV century by Juan de Contreras is also worth seeing.

PEDRAZA

A charming village some 35 kilometres from Segovia. Pedraza is highly
picturesque and built on an imposing rock, surrounded by its walls and
with only one entrance; it has many hidden corners and secluded squares
with lordly mansions reminding us of the past.

Its most outstanding monuments are the XV century castle which rises up
out of a grove of trees on the edge of the rock with its high tower where the
painter Ignacio Zuloaga had his studio, and the lovely porticoed Plaza Mayor overlooked by the Romanesque outline of the tower of San Juan.

Pedraza was the domain of the Constables of Castile. The town contends
with Italica over the honour of being the birth place of Trajan; it was here
where the children of Henry II of France were kept prisoner.

*Three views of the historical town of
Pedraza.*

A typical street in Pedraza.

A magnificent close up of the castle at Turégano rising up impressively over the elegant porticoed town square whose past episcopal splendour has left illustrious traces throughout the double towered precinct.

PRADENA

A picturesque town near Navafría where the most exquisite trout are fished; it has an impressive church with a neoclassical façade, and a recently discovered enormous grotto is an attraction for the tourist.

TUREGANO

A pretty village some 34 kilometres from Segovia, whose most characteristic view is that of its porticoed square and its castle rising up in the distance. In this castle segovian bishops fortified the Romanesque church of Saint Michael and surrounded it with a turreted precinct. Turégano reached the height of its splendour at the end of the XV century and don Juan Arias-Dávila was the instigator of its most important buildings.

Remains are still left of the city wall round the castle; apparently the wall belonged to a previous fortress, possibly XII century. Another interesting monument in Turégano is the church of Santiago. The village has a mediaeval personality and many of its streets are narrow and winding, flanked by typically mediaeval buildings.

Antonio Pérez, the famous secretary of Philip II was a prisoner in the castle of Turégano.

On saying goodbye to Segovia one is filled with many differing memories and overwhelmed by nostalgia. The intimate human character of the city with its handsome monuments make up a real gift for the spirit and a stimulus to the sensibility. Segovia is engraved forever in our memory as a friendly image which we fervently desire to see again. Segovia is a city one always needs to return to.

A poetical general view of Segovia taken from the Roman aqueduct at dawn.

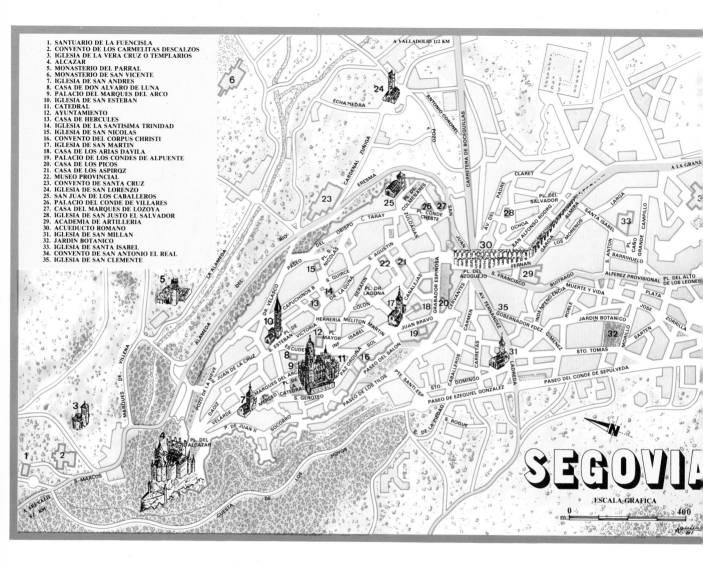

SEGOVIA

ESCALA GRAFICA

Contents

Collection ALL EUROPE

	Spanish	French	English	German	Italian	Catalan	Dutch	Swedish	Portuguese	Japanese	Arab
1 ANDORRA	■	■	■	■	□	■	□	■	□	□	□
2 LISBON	■	■	■	■	■	□	□	■	■	□	□
3 LONDON	■	■	■	■	■	□	□	■	□	□	□
4 BRUGES	■	■	■	■	■	□	■	□	□	□	□
5 PARIS	■	■	■	■	■	□	□	□	■	□	□
6 MONACO	■	■	■	■	■	□	□	□	□	□	□
7 VIENNA	■	■	■	■	■	■	□	□	■	■	□
8 NICE	■	■	■	■	■	□	□	□	□	□	□
9 CANNES	■	■	■	■	■	□	□	□	□	□	□
10 ROUSSILLON	■	■	■	■	■	□	□	■	■	□	□
11 VERDUN	■	■	■	■	■	□	□	□	□	□	□
12 THE TOWER OF LONDON	■	■	■	■	■	□	□	□	□	□	□
13 ANTWERP	■	■	■	■	■	□	□	□	□	□	□
14 WESTMINSTER ABBEY	■	■	■	■	■	□	□	□	□	□	□
15 THE SPANISH RIDING SCHOOL IN VIENNA	■	■	■	■	■	□	□	□	□	□	□
16 FATIMA	■	■	■	■	■	□	□	□	■	□	□
17 WINDSOR CASTLE	■	■	■	■	■	□	□	□	■	□	□
18 THE OPAL COAST	□	■	■	■	■	□	□	□	□	□	□
19 COTE D'AZUR	■	■	■	■	■	□	□	□	□	□	□
20 AUSTRIA	■	■	■	■	■	□	□	□	□	□	□
21 LOURDES	■	■	■	■	□	□	□	□	□	□	□
22 BRUSSELS	■	■	■	■	□	■	□	■	□	□	□

Collection ALL AMERICA

	Spanish	French	English	German	Italian	Catalan	Dutch	Swedish	Portuguese	Japanese	Arab
1 PUERTO RICO	■	□	■	□	□	□	□	□	□	□	□
2 SANTO DOMINGO	■	□	■	□	□	□	□	□	□	□	□

Collection ALL AFRICA

	Spanish	French	English	German	Italian	Catalan	Dutch	Swedish	Portuguese	Japanese	Arab
1 MOROCCO	■	■	■	■	□	□	□	□	□	□	■

Collection ART IN SPAIN

	Spanish	French	English	German	Italian	Catalan	Dutch	Swedish	Portuguese	Japanese	Arab
1 PALAU DE LA MUSICA CATALANA (Catalan Palace of Music)	■	■	■	■	□	■	□	□	□	□	□
2 GAUDI	■	■	■	■	□	□	□	□	□	□	□
3 PRADO MUSEUM I (Spanish Painting)	■	■	■	■	■	□	□	□	□	■	□
4 PRADO MUSEUM II (Foreign Painting)	■	■	■	■	■	□	□	□	□	□	□
5 THE ROOF-BOSSES OF THE CATHEDRAL OF GERONA	■	□	□	□	□	□	□	□	□	□	□
6 THE CASTLE OF XAVIER	■	□	□	□	□	□	□	□	□	□	□
7 THE ROMANESQUE STYLE IN SPAIN	■	■	■	□	□	□	□	□	□	□	□
8 SPANISH CASTLES	■	■	■	□	□	□	□	□	□	□	□
9 THE CATHEDRALS OF SPAIN	■	■	■	■	□	□	□	□	□	□	□
10 THE CATHEDRAL OF GERONA	■	■	■	■	□	□	□	□	□	□	□
11 GRAN TEATRO DEL LICEO DE BARCELONA (The Great Opera House)	■	■	■	■	■	■	□	□	□	□	□
12 THE ROMANESQUE STYLE IN CATALONIA	■	■	■	□	□	□	□	□	□	□	□
13 LA RIOJA: ART TREASURES AND WINE-GROWING RESOURCES	■	■	■	■	□	□	□	□	□	□	□
14 PICASSO	■	■	■	■	□	□	□	□	□	□	□
15 THE BAROQUE STYLE IN SPAIN	■	■	■	□	□	□	□	□	□	□	□
16 ROMAN REMAINS IN SPAIN	■	■	■	□	□	□	□	□	□	□	□
17 THE GOTHIC STYLE IN SPAIN	■	■	■	□	□	□	□	□	□	□	□
18 THE WINES OF CATALONIA	■	■	■	■	□	□	□	□	□	□	□
19 THE ALHAMBRA AND THE GENERALIFE	■	■	■	■	□	□	□	□	□	□	□
20 GRANADA AND THE ALHAMBRA (ARAB AND MAURESQUE MONUMENTS OF CORDOVA, SEVILLE AND GRANADA)	■	□	□	□	□	□	□	□	□	□	□

Collection ALL SPAIN

	Spanish	French	English	German	Italian	Catalan	Dutch	Swedish	Portuguese	Japanese	Arab
1 ALL MADRID	■	■	■	■	■	□	□	□	□	□	■
2 ALL BARCELONA	■	■	■	■	■	■	□	□	□	□	□
3 ALL SEVILLE	■	■	■	■	■	□	□	□	■	□	□
4 ALL MAJORCA	■	■	■	■	■	□	□	□	□	□	□
5 ALL THE COSTA BRAVA	■	■	■	■	□	□	□	□	□	□	□
6 ALL MALAGA and the Costa del Sol	■	■	■	■	□	□	□	□	□	□	□
7 ALL THE CANARY ISLANDS I, Lanzarote and Fuerteventura	■	■	■	■	□	□	■	□	□	□	□
8 ALL CORDOBA	■	■	■	■	■	□	□	□	□	□	□
9 ALL GRANADA	■	■	■	■	■	□	□	□	■	□	□
10 ALL VALENCIA	■	■	■	■	□	□	□	□	□	□	□
11 ALL TOLEDO	■	■	■	■	■	□	□	□	□	□	□
12 ALL SANTIAGO and the Rías Bajas	■	■	■	■	□	□	□	□	□	□	□
13 ALL IBIZA and Formentera	■	■	■	■	□	□	□	□	□	□	□
14 ALL CADIZ and the Costa de la Luz	■	■	■	■	□	□	□	□	□	□	□
15 ALL MONTSERRAT	■	■	■	■	□	□	□	□	□	□	□
16 ALL SANTANDER and the Costa Esmeralda	■	■	■	□	□	□	□	□	□	□	□
17 ALL THE CANARY ISLANDS II, Tenerife, La Palma, Gomera, Hierro	■	■	■	■	□	□	■	□	□	□	□
18 ALL PEÑISCOLA	■	■	■	■	□	□	□	□	□	□	□
19 ALL SITGES	■	■	■	■	□	□	□	□	□	□	□
20 ALL BURGOS, Covarrubias and Santo Domingo de Silos	■	■	■	□	□	□	□	□	□	□	□
21 ALL ALICANTE and the Costa Blanca	■	■	■	■	□	□	■	□	□	□	□
22 ALL NAVARRA	■	■	■	□	□	□	□	□	□	□	□
23 ALL LERIDA Province and Pyrenees	■	■	■	■	□	■	□	□	□	□	□
24 ALL SEGOVIA and Province	■	■	■	■	□	□	□	□	□	□	□
25 ALL SARAGOSSA and Province	■	■	■	■	□	□	□	□	□	□	□
26 ALL SALAMANCA and Province	■	■	■	■	□	□	□	■	□	□	□
27 ALL AVILA and Province	■	■	■	■	□	□	□	□	□	□	□
28 ALL MINORCA	■	■	■	■	□	□	□	□	□	□	□
29 ALL SAN SEBASTIAN and Province	■	■	■	■	□	□	□	□	□	□	□
30 ALL ASTURIAS	■	■	■	■	□	□	□	□	□	□	□
31 ALL CORUNNA and the Rías Altas	■	■	■	■	□	□	□	□	□	□	□
32 ALL TARRAGONA and Province	■	■	■	■	□	□	□	□	□	□	□
33 ALL MURCIA and Province	■	■	■	■	□	□	□	□	□	□	□
34 ALL VALLADOLID and Province	■	■	■	■	□	□	□	□	□	□	□
35 ALL GIRONA and Province	■	■	■	■	□	□	□	□	□	□	□
36 ALL HUESCA and Province	■	■	■	□	□	□	□	□	□	□	□
37 ALL JAEN and Province	■	■	■	□	□	□	□	□	□	□	□
38 ALL ALMERIA and Province	■	■	■	□	□	□	□	□	□	□	□
39 ALL CASTELLON and the Costa del Azahar	■	■	■	■	□	□	□	□	□	□	□
40 ALL CUENCA and Province	■	■	■	□	□	□	□	□	□	□	□
41 ALL LEON and Province	■	■	■	□	□	□	□	□	□	□	□
42 ALL PONTEVEDRA, VIGO and the Rías Bajas	■	■	■	■	□	□	□	□	□	□	□
43 ALL RONDA	■	■	■	■	□	□	□	□	□	□	□
44 ALL SORIA	■	□	□	□	□	□	□	□	□	□	□

FUENTIDUEÑA

Pantano de Linares

MADERUELO

CUELLAR

AYL

Pantano de Burguillo

SEPULVEDA

CASTILNOVO

Río Cega

RIAZA

COCA

NAVA DE
LA ASUNCION

TUREGANO

PEDRAZA

Somosierra

Río

SANTA MARIA
LA REAL DE NIEVA

PRADENA

Srra. de Guadarrama

Eresma

MARTIN MUÑOZ

SEGOVIA

LA GRANJA

RIOFRIO

VILLACASTIN

Navacerrada

Alto de los Leones

FRANCIA

PORTUGAL

ISLAS BALEARES

ISLAS CANARIAS

The printing of this book was completed
in the workshops of FISA - Industrias
Gráficas, Palaudarias, 26 - Barcelona
(Spain)